Harley-Davidson
in the 1960s

Allan Girdler and Jeff Hackett

MBI Publishing Company

First published in 2001 by MBI Publishing Company
Galtier Plaza, Suite 200, 380 Jackson Street,
St. Paul, MN 55101-3885 USA.

MBI Publishing Company books are also available at
discounts in bulk quantity for industrial or sales-promotional
use. For details write to Special Sales Manager at
Motorbooks International Wholesalers & Distributors
Galtier Plaza, Suite 200, 380 Jackson Street,
St. Paul, MN 55101-3885 USA.

Library of Congress Cataloging-in-Publication
Data Available.

ISBN 0-7603-1058-0

On the front cover: This was the perfect performance profile,
with skinny fenders and peanut tank emphasizing the muscle
of the engine. The now-classic hamcan air cleaner covers the
floatless Tillotson carburetor, above the magneto ignition.
The carb and mag were both temperamental, which added
to the appeal of the model. *Owner: David Carlton*

On the frontispiece: The Sprint's horizontal four-stroke single
and left-side kick-start were conventional Italian practice, as
was the mechanical tachometer driven off the gearcase. The
box labeled Sprint H contains the tools.

On the title page: In 1963 the AMA allowed the use of
fairings for road races. This is a 1963 KRTT, the side-valve
KR engine fitted with suspension and brakes, with larger
fuel and oil tanks, a skimpy, streamlined seat, and a fairing,
all from the Harley-Davidson parts book.
Owner: Keith Campbell

On the back cover: By the time the electric leg was debugged
in 1966, the Panhead top end was replaced by the
Shovelhead, which had improved breathing and added
power. *Owner: Rick Newman*

Edited by Darwin Holmstrom
Designed by Tom Heffron

Printed in China

CONTENTS

INTRODUCTION

An ad in the February 1960 issue of *American Motorcyclist*, official publication of the American Motorcyclist Association (AMA), reads:

LIKE MOTORCYCLES AND MONEY?

Then send for Harley-Davidson Dealership book on how to become a franchised dealer of motorcycles and a new line of motor scooters. Here's a chance to own your own business with a very modest investment. The Youth Market is beginning to explode and the next few years promise a chance to cash in on it.

Note the key buzzwords, "youth market," and the steel warning wrapped in the warm and fuzzy promise.

Chance.

But don't worry, this story has an improbably happy ending. At the same time it's real history, so real that as poet Randall Jarrell says about something entirely different: you had to see it *not* to believe it.

The story has several beginnings.

First, one of the inconvenient delights of taking history seriously is that facts don't always fit the format. For instance, the Hundred Years' War began in 1337 and ended in 1453. Like that conflict, some eras are too big for their format. The events that give shape to the era we call the 1960s began before and finished after that decade.

Second, taking history seriously means finding new facts, which often contradict and challenge earlier opinions. In the case of Harley-Davidson in the 1960s, at least four such challenges arise, generated by detailed examination.

Third, when F. Scott Fitzgerald wrote "There are no second acts in American lives," he didn't mean we don't get to try again. We do. His reference was to the rules of drama. In the classic three-act play, expectations are raised in act one, confounded in act two, and resolved in act three.

So it will be here. Without giving away the happy ending or the dramatic turns of events Harley-Davidson during this time was as creative and disruptive as was the era itself.

Fourth, the beginning of the era isn't the beginning of the story.

When The Motor Company, as insiders call Harley-Davidson, published that ad inviting investors to get in on the fun and the action, it had ample reason for the confidence that invitation displays.

Harley-Davidson's Duo-Glide was the Motor Company's top-of-the-line model at the dawn of the 1960s.

PROLOGUE

Harley-Davidson began at the turn of the twentieth century, when Arthur Davidson and William Harley realized they could do more fishing, hunting, and roaming around if their bicycles had engines.

No one in their Milwaukee, Wisconsin, neighborhood had motorcycles. Neither Davidson nor Harley could afford the machines, not on the money they made as a pattern maker and a fitter, respectively.

But the two men were smart, industrious, and mechanically inclined. With the help of the two other Davidson brothers, Walter and William, they made a bicycle with a very basic four-stroke, single-cylinder engine. Then they took it a step further and made a real motorcycle that was larger and stronger and had a bigger and improved engine.

Harley and the Davidsons went into business in 1903 and called the company Harley-Davidson despite the ratio of three Davidsons to one Harley because it sounded best.

Harley-Davidson became a textbook success story for the next 50 years. The founders were honest and delivered a good product for the money. The four turned out to be a good fit: William Harley was a sound and practical engineer; William Davidson was a natural leader and a perfect choice to run the plant; Walter Davidson was a natural rider and businessman; and Arthur Davidson was born to sell. Each talent was needed and appreciated.

At the time Harley-Davidson incorporated in 1907, scores, if not hundreds, of motorcycle makers existed in the United States and Europe.

Harley-Davidson started small, but made the correct choices. Indian Motorcycle Manufacturing Company, the

To compete with the flood of small-displacement Japanese motorcycles that were taking over the U.S. market in the 1960s, Harley built lightweight singles at its Aermacchi plant in Italy. The Sprint, introduced to the American market in 1961, was the first of the Aermacchi machines to be badged as a Harley-Davidson.
Owner: Ted Tine, Essex Motorsports

largest motorcycle manufacturer in the 1910s, didn't make such good choices. When Indian needed money to expand, the founders sold stock to the banks. Before you knew it, the banks were in charge and had retired the founders.

When Harley-Davidson needed money the company borrowed, but kept the stock and paid back the loans.

When World War I arrived, Indian's bankers even eliminated the middlemen, the dealers, and sold all their products directly to the military. Harley supported the war effort, but kept civilian models in production. When the war ended and the boys came home with money saved, Harley-Davidson had a dealer network and Indian didn't. Harley-Davidson became the big guy.

During the Great Depression, Harley-Davidson introduced a sporting middleweight, the Model E, affectionately known since as the "Knucklehead." Indian revised its up market Four. One move was good, one bad.

At the finish of World War II, Indian's new managers put all their eggs in the new basket, so to speak, introducing new models that didn't work well and didn't sell.

Here's the first contradiction. When The Motor Company was at its lowest point (much later in its history) critics said it was because Harley-Davidson had restricted itself to big bikes and ignored the rest of the market.

That wasn't the case. In 1947 Harley built the 125 cc two-stroke single, best known as the "Hummer." But Harley continued making big twins and middleweight twins, counting on the buyers who prefer old machines to wrong machines.

When the market grew, so did Harley-Davidson. When the public wanted something new, Harley-Davidson was ready, or so the company thought.

The Italian-built Sprints weren't enough to stop Honda from becoming the number one motorcycle company in the United States, but they did achieve success on U.S. racetracks. *Owner: Tom Sephton*

Expectations Are Raised

HARLEY ENTERS THE DECADE ON A HIGH NOTE

The Sportster, introduced in 1957, was a big little bike; a middleweight styled to look like a smaller version of the flagship FLH but with a much-improved overhead valve, 54-cid V-twin. *Owner: Don Chasteen*

Perhaps because deep down Harley-Davidson executives and spokesmen knew they were playing catch-up, sometimes major advances didn't get much ink.

Just before the 1960s began, motorcycling in America was much smaller and very different from what it came to be.

How small? In 1959 slightly more than 500,000 motorcycles were registered in the United States. About 70,000 riders belonged to the AMA, the only national group and racing's sanctioning body and the only place the motorcycle factories could meet as well as compete. Perhaps 100,000 riders read the few national magazines devoted to the sport, and when television or a mass-media publication mentioned bikes, the cycle crowd was both surprised and pleased.

The open road existed and was a challenge. About 800 riders rode to the rally and dirt track races in Sturgis, South Dakota, in 1959. By the year 2000, an estimated 650,000 people went to Sturgis. (Finding a seat at the

By 1960 the Duo-Glide was state-of-the-art: It was big, with room for two on the sprung seat, suspension front and rear, and available with a windshield, fiberglass saddlebags, chrome-plated case guards, and even a luggage rack. *Owner: Joe Osborne*

races was still easy because so many people were busy buying or ogling T-shirts, or loading their just-bought machines into trailers for the tow home.)

The Big Twins

Harley-Davidson's big sellers at the time and since the end of the war were the big twins.

Harley's major model line began with that Knucklehead, the Model E in 1936. The E engine became the F when it grew from 61 ci to 74 ci, and then was joined by the FL, a slightly more powerful version with a higher compression ratio.

Why did L stand for higher? Nobody knows. In 1948 Harley replaced the cast-iron cylinder head of the Knucklehead engine with aluminum alloy heads, earning the engine the nickname "Panhead." A year later the F and FL got hydraulic front forks, giving birth to the name "Hydra-Glide." The foot clutch pedal and hand gearshift were swapped for a hand-controlled clutch and foot-shifted gearbox, but Harley-Davidson didn't want to scare

The Duo-Glide, in this case a 1964, presents what has become the classic profile of a big motorcycle. The winged "H" on the oil tank signifies an FLH, which featured the tuned engine. The chromed rectangle below the leading edge of the fuel tank is a helper spring—known as a "mousetrap"—to allow hand operation of a foot-powered clutch. *Owner: Tim Beitler*

off the rational riders, so order books offered an FL with a hand shift and an FLF for foot shift. Oh yeah, some police departments missed the old mild tune of the side-valve engines, so there was an option of the FLE, E here meaning the mildest possible camshaft timing.

Oh yeah again, because of a market for sidecars, Harley-Davidson offered an optional gearbox with reverse, coded FLS.

Still in the history section, engineers developed more power for the Panhead, which could run cooler and thus longer at speed. They also beefed up the engine's lower end and gave special attention to the heads. The resulting motorcycle was offered as the FLH.

Perhaps the most important option offered with the FLH was the "King of the Highway" package.

It doesn't sound like much but the package consisted of extra chrome, a full-sized windshield that bolted to the front suspension, plastic saddlebags, replacing leather because Harley-Davidson had a plastics division and leather isn't all that good in the rain and sun. Extras were part of the sport for years, in the form of heavy coats and windscreens, but this

From an electrical perspective, the 1964 Duo-Glide was the most reliable of the Panheads. The 1965 Electra Glide, the last of the Panheads and the first Harley Big Twin to receive an electric starter, had a few wiring gremlins. *Owner: David Kiesow*

The Duo-Glide's engine space is a busy place. This 1964 motorcycle carries an oil cooler on the case guard, thus the lines to and from the oil tank. The little gadget beneath the horn's trumpet is the ignition timer and the chromed housing aft of the oil tank is the toolbox. *Owner: Essex Motorsports*

The FLH's optional windscreen was basic but effective, as was the steering damper just in front of the speedometer. FLH tanks are separate, left and right joined by a hidden hose, and the paint on this pair on a 1964 model differ because the bike is not restored and now has two shades of original paint. *Owner: Essex Motorsports*

was formal recognition of motorcycle touring as a package from the factory.

In 1958 the F series, the big twins, gained rear suspension and a new name: Duo-Glide. Harley-Davidson's ads divided the models into the three classes and showed the FLH as a full touring rig, but they didn't proclaim the rear swing arm and shocks, surely because the smaller Harleys, and the imports from across both oceans, had offered full suspensions for years before that.

Not that it mattered all that much, but in 1964, when *Cycle World* introduced its accurate and unbiased road test to motorcycling, the magazine explained that yes, the FLH was large, heavy, and not especially fast or nimble. The FLH was made "for those for whom the lightweights, however fast and agile, are just toys."

According to the test, the FLH had a 61-inch wheelbase, weighed 690 pounds with the 3.75-gallon tanks half full, did the standing-start quarter mile in 15.8 seconds

As H-D's top-of-the-line model, the FLH appealed to the man who wanted everything. The factory agreed, as seen on this 1965 model with the dual exhausts (never mind that both cylinders also fed into the right side muffler). The odd object below the sprung solo saddle is a helper spring for riders with large, uh, appetites. *Owner: Frank Vespa, Classic Cycles*

and had a practical top speed, as clocked after a half-mile run, of 97 miles per hour.

Harley-Davidson policy then was to build as many machines as the dealers could sell: Twice each year they took the orders, and then filled the demand.

What that meant was Harley-Davidson built about 6,000 big twins, nearly 3,000 Sportsters, and maybe 2,500 lightweights and a handful of racing models and Servi-cars, the three-wheelers service stations, car dealers, and Motor Maids used.

If that doesn't sound like much, remember that Harley-Davidson was by far the largest company in the field in the United States.

Sportsters

With The Motor Company being the largest tiger in the two-wheeled jungle, a magazine ran a photo of Harley-Davidson's "second-generation management team."

William H. Davidson was company president, Gordon Davidson was vice president for manufacturing, William J. Harley was vice president for engineering, and Walter C. Davidson was vice president of sales. The four

Buyers could pick and choose options. For instance, this FLH has the fiberglass saddlebags—okay, they're boxes, not bags, but we still call them saddlebags—but lacks the windshield. Collectors now call bikes equipped like this "bare baggers." *Owner: Tom Mahar*

But wait, there was more. A popular way to stand out in the crowd in the early 1960s was to add all the lights the bike could carry, literally. Sure, flipping all the switches drained the battery in seconds, but it was a light show while it lasted.

men were filling their dads' offices. They did a pretty fair job, albeit there must have been some favoritism, not to say nepotism, involved in their careers.

What looked best, though, at the start of the 1960s, was the middleweight class, home of the Sportster. This was part accident, part footwork, and part intelligence. After World War II, imports took hold in the U.S. market, especially the English marques. They offered sports models with modern features like overhead valves, foot shift, and suspension front and rear.

Harley-Davidson countered with a compromise: the old side-valve 45-cid V-twin, combined with unit construction, crankcase and gearbox in the same housing, plus telescopic front forks, swing arm rear suspension, and foot shift on the right, just like the Triumphs and Nortons and in contrast to the big Harley twins, which had their gear levers on the left.

The XL arrived with a large fuel tank, full fenders, and options like the case guards and luggage rack shown here on a 1958 Sportster. *Owner: Don Chasteen*

The side valve engine was the weak part. In 1957 that model, the KH, was replaced by the XL Sportster, which had the same 54-cid displacement as the KH, but with larger bore, shorter stroke, and enough power to meet and defeat the imports.

Here's the deft part. It was the era of big and flashy cars, Oldsmobiles and Dodges as big as Cadillacs and Lincolns. Harley's planners figured what the middleweight crowd wanted was sort of a smaller FLH. The first XL was that, with enclosing (valanced, in designer terms) fenders, a big fuel tank, and a sturdy profile.

The launch went moderately well, except that (this was recounted orally, and isn't in the Harley-Davidson official version) the California dealers said they needed something to compete in amateur, off-road events.

It happened that a closed-circuit class called TT with jumps and turns in both directions was part of the pro circuit. Harley-Davidson offered a model, the KHRTT, for that class and had the full race, on- or off-road model, called the KR.

Pause here for some jargon. Ever since Harley adopted letters for model designations, the model was initially (sorry) one letter: J for the basic V-twin with lights, F for the same bike with magneto ignition and no lights. Sometimes the engine would be made larger or better, in which case the new version was the JD or the JH. Or a second stage of tune, with higher compression ratio or larger carburetor, model would be in the EL or the WL series.

The point here is that the factory used these same letters as an ordering or internal code and most of the time they didn't stand for anything else. (This changed 50 years later.)

Back to the Sportster. The engineering department was also ready with a TT bike, the XLR. The R of course stands for racing. The XLR combined the XL's frame, brakes, suspension, and the XL engine's overhead-valve top end with the lower end from the sidevalve KR, which featured ball bearing main bearings and camshaft bearings, special oil pump, and magneto ignition. The fuel tank was the cute little (2.5 gal) version first used on the 125cc Hummer and later borrowed for the KR. And the XLR, formally the XLRTT—in Harleyspeak TT means a race

bike with rear suspension—also used the low, separate straight pipes from the KR. Harley didn't advertise the XLR because its full-race engine was considered too fragile for the general public. Therefore, when the California dealers wanted a play bike for the off-road crowd, the factory did another classic H-D blend. In 1958 the XL and XLR were joined by the XLC, an XL stripped of lights and with bobbed fenders, the little fuel tank now known as the Peanut tank, a KR magneto, and those low and separate straight pipes.

The X-series engine proved even stronger than expected. In addition to the XL, and the XLC and XLR, Harley offered a tuned version with a higher compression ratio and the letters XLH.

The letter H is part of the factory code and had been for 30-plus years when the XLH tune became an option. The reporter who did the new-model story didn't know this and wrote the H should stand for hot. Years later Harley-Davidson's ad agency used the line and, however inaccurate the saying, it became part of the company's lore.

The junior version of the XL was selling well, and the sports models, the XLC and even more so the XLCH, the lean machine with the small tank, tiny headlight, and race-based magneto ignition, created a new market.

It was the dawn of the superbike, a mass-produced high-performance motorcycle and the most bang for your buck.

Sure, a 1953 Vincent Black Shadow as it came from the factory probably had motor on a stock 1960 XLCH, but nobody much cared because none of the faithful had ever seen a Vincent.

Those of us with Hummers, Triumph Cubs, Mustangs (bargain-basement scooters), clapped-out side valve Harleys, or leaky old BSAs knew that the XLCH was fast and we knew guys who had them were usually the guys our moms feared would try to date our sisters. This is a long way of saying the XLCH was the bike to have.

The Motor Company in those days had no problem with "Not Invented Here." If that's what the public wanted, fine. And Harley always had an open option department, so the buyer could have the big tank on his XLCH or the solo seat and small tank with the

The XL engine shifted on the right, like the rival English middleweights, rather than on the left, like the FLH. The Sportster's only technical shortcoming was that the ohv heads were cast iron, not more efficient alloy. *Owner: Don Chasteen*

The Stripper XLC sold so well that for 1959 the factory offered the XLCH, the first mass-produced superbike, with the upgraded H-designated engine, a racing magneto ignition, barely muffled exhaust pipes, a small headlight, and the peanut tank used by the dirt track racers. *Owner: Dave Georgiano*

full-fendered and battery-ignited XLH. In any case, in 1959 they made (and sold presumably) 947 XLHs and 1,059 XLCHs, and they all were conquest sales to riders who otherwise would have bought a Norton, Triumph, Royal Enfield, or BSA.

What did they get? Performance is as relative as anything else, but a 1962 *Cycle World* test reported that an XLCH was "clearly the fastest mass-produced motorcycle we have had."

The figures were 14.3 seconds for the standing-start quarter mile and a top speed of 122 miles per hour. Curb weight was 480 pounds, with a wheelbase of 57 inches. By the standards of the day, quoting CW's test again, "There

The XLCH—seen here as a 1959 example with more chrome than it had when it was new—was as raw and aggressive as it sounded and looked. With an engine barely contained by its frame, the XLCH created and captured the performance bike market. *Owner: Cliff Nelms*

Speaking of something completely different, the Topper scooter was neat, if not chic. This is the (relatively) high performance version, as revealed by the "H" emblem on the fairing. Also visible are the leading-link front suspension, the handle for the pull start (just above the footwell on the rider's right), and the passenger's folding foot pedal, just about the only motorcycle part on the scooter. *Owner: Fred Hundertfund*

sure is a lot of it . . . the fastest thing an expert rider is likely to find for sale anywhere, and when that is said, everything else is superfluous."

Lightweights

The Sportster was serendipity, a happy accident, and Harley-Davidson's managers had every reason to take advantage of their luck.

But the real credit for doing the right thing comes from a scooter.

Yes indeed. Hard though it is to believe now, a worldwide scooter fad hit at about the same time as a motorcycle revival. With world economies recovering, scooters became good urban tools popular in Italy,

The Topper scooter, with fiberglass bodywork, automatic transmission, toaster-oven styling, and tiny wheels, was as far from an FLH as you can get on two wheels. But it sold well, at first, anyway. *Owner: Fred Hundertfund*

The 125-cc two-stroke, here in 1959 form, was as basic and unHarley as the Topper, but in its own way.

The 125's fuel tank is the only shape still familiar to Harley fans, as the little tank was borrowed for the dirt-track racers and then the XLCH.

Germany, England, and Japan. The makers there saw opportunity in the United States.

When Harley-Davidson was in trouble later, some critics said it was because the company was too specialized, making only big two-cylinder motorcycles and neglecting the rest of the market.

This is nonsense. Harley-Davidson began with practical singles, then expanded into the classic twins, but there was even a short run of pedal bicycles, with the famous bar and shield. The singles were in the catalog all through the 1930s.

More to this point, in 1947, when transportation was in short supply but prosperity had returned, Harley introduced a two-stroke, 125 cc single, a basic motorcycle designed for the youth market. That phrase was part of The Motor Company's vocabulary even then.

The 125 cc grew into a 165 cc and was offered in street, dirt, and dual-sport forms, and the little bikes were advertised right along with the full-dress FLH.

Harley-Davidson was aware of trends, so when scooters arrived the engineers in Milwaukee modified the company's two-stroke engine to accept a pull starter, rubber engine mounts, and an automatic transmission. "Scootaway," the ads proclaimed, when the Topper was introduced.

This was major news, so much so that *American Motorcyclist* put Bert and Bart Maverick, stars of a TV western series, on the cover, two-up, heading off to the golf course.

Not quite the outlaw image someone might expect. And this was when Honda, famous now for introducing nice people to one another, advertised "An Avalanche of Unsurpassable Competition Victories."

Clearly the emphasis on speed and power didn't do Honda any harm, but equally, Harley-Davidson's efforts to broaden their customer base were working, too.

Official production figures for the 1960 model year show the Duo-Glide (by this time nearly all in FLH form) at 5,967 machines. Sportster total was 2,765. The lightweights added to 2,488, Servi-cars were 7,078, and Topper sales came to 3,801.

Clearly, the scooter was a good move.

As a footnote to that, several states made allowances for kids who needed transportation. Riders between 14 and 16 were allowed to operate scooters, mopeds, and small motorcycles with less than 5 bhp. Harley and

The 125's rear wheel was bolted to the frame. Why was the horn back there? Probably because there was room.

most other factories used restrictors in the intake manifold, just as NASCAR does on speedways, so there was the Topper A, and the restricted AU. In 1961 the Topper got a power boost, higher compression ratio and 9 bhp, so like the XL, the A became the AH.

Footnoting that, of course, as farms became housing tracts and young operators became suspects, the states went from empowerment to making licensing as difficult as possible. Sorry, kids. Those of us who were kids then took maybe two days to yank the restrictors, bringing the long arm of the law down on you later.

Here's a hint as chapter one comes to a close, the smaller models had problems.

One was that some of the dealers and even Harley owners weren't that pleased to see kids and their little bikes hanging around the shop.

Next, right after the introduction of the little 125 cc, the English pound sterling was devalued; the United Kingdom was in serious financial trouble.

The Harley Hummer and the BSA Bantam were both based on the pre-war DKW, same basic engine. But now the BSA was a lot cheaper than the Hummer, which meant in the short run that selling Hummers was difficult, and in the long run the price of an American-made motorcycle competing with European or Japanese motorcycles became a problem.

So without making a big fuss, Harley-Davidson's managers did some shopping of their own, and bought into an Italian motorcycle company, Aermacchi, which loosely translated means "air machine." The company made airplanes before getting into the motorcycle business.

In the early 1960s, Harley-Davidson had all the bases covered.

The little single was tidy and efficient, if not fast. Kick-start and shift levers are both on the left, with a toolbox mounted behind them.

Expectations Are Confounded

HARLEY LOSES THE LEAD

Chrome-plated extras were as popular then as they are now. Notice all the covers and scoops. The factory devised a way to route the Shovelhead's second exhaust pipe around the starter, which allowed for the second, symmetrical muffler. *Owner: Rick Newman*

Early in the corporation's history, and as mentioned in the first chapter, The Motor Company's founders expanded the operation with borrowed money but kept the ownership firmly in the families.

Compared to Indian's history, this was a good decision, but as circumstances and the world changed, this became a matter of great importance to the company's survival.

The nature of closely held, private, or family firms means that the founding fathers' children, not to mention extended family, must feel pressure to keep the dividends coming. What stockholders sometimes forget is that a firm may need to invest in the future, as in research and development, and new and improved plants. This became critical when the nature of motorcycling changed.

There's a lot more here than meets a first glance. The 1965 FLH, the last of the Panheads, is the first model designated an Electra Glide. The kick-start was retained, but the new electric starter, requiring a much larger battery, eliminated the toolbox. *Owner: Tom Mahar*

The AMA magazine then always included a page or two devoted to the Motor Maids, women who rode motorcycles and a club whose rules allowed for expulsion of any woman caught towing her machine on a trailer to an event. Clubs held annual contests for the most popular boy and girl—yes, they were called that—riders. Club members wore uniforms, paramilitary style, and rallies included best-dressed club competitions and ride-the-plank contests.

The AMA magazine also had a section devoted to dealership names and addresses. This was so riders on motorcycles that broke down on the road could better find people who would help. The two-page directories could be folded and tucked away, just in case.

Most of the dealerships listed were Harley shops. The listings for those that weren't usually stated, "All makes and models welcome."

Motorcycling in the early 1960s was parochial, close knit, and maybe even insular, all of which became subject to pressure and to change.

The Big Twins

On the subject of change, Harley-Davidson was famous for evolution even before the Evolution name was attached to a Harley engine.

In 1965, only five years after Honda and peers proved that motorcycles could offer an electric start and that riders liked it, Harley-Davidson introduced the Electra Glide, with a starter button, a bigger battery, 50 or so more pounds, and a great relief.

(Usage note: Harley-Davidson has always insisted on the hyphen between Harley and Davidson but otherwise, there's no clear rule. The FL series has been the Hydra-Glide,

then the Duo-Glide in the factory's ads and brochures, but in 1965 it was the Electra Glide, right next to the Servi-Car. No reason was given. That's just how it's done.)

(Historical note: Often credit for Harley's first electric start is given to the Electra Glide of 1965, but the Servi-car got the electric leg in 1964. Servi-cars weren't considered motorcycles, so the facts got lost, but it's a safe way to win bets at the corner tavern.)

The next major improvement came in 1966 when the "Panhead" top end was replaced by the "Shovelhead."

The electric starter is visible below the seat and above the primary drive cover. The starter drive spun the gearbox's input sprocket, pulling the primary chain, and turning the engine. Mounting the starter there eliminated the second exhaust pipe and muffler. *Owner: Tom Mahar*

The Panhead FLHE (E for electric) was the top-of-the-line model and usually came with the other options, such as saddlebags, trim, and windshield. The starting system added at least 75 pounds to an already large machine. *Owner: Tom Mahar*

The nicknames seem to exist because riders and owners like getting personal. The earlier Knucklehead was so called because the nuts on the rocker covers looked like knuckles. The Panhead is supposed to resemble a cake pan, and the Shovelhead resembles, if you look at it a little sideways and squint, the business end of a coal shovel.

The beefed-up FLH version of the Panhead was strong enough to hold up under more power, which justified the even better breathing Shovelhead. In like manner, after

By the time the electric leg was debugged in 1966, the Panhead top end was replaced by the Shovelhead, which had improved breathing and added power. *Owner: Rick Newman*

This was the perfect performance profile, with skinny fenders and peanut tank emphasizing the muscle of the engine. The now-classic hamcan air cleaner covers the floatless Tillotson carburetor, above the magneto ignition. The carb and mag were both temperamental, which added to the appeal of the model. *Owner: David Carlton*

solving the teething problems of the initially troublesome electric start, the engine could be upgraded.

The motorcycle had one drawback, except maybe for the added weight. The larger battery and the electric motor took away room for a tool box, which had been on Harleys since the 1910s and which, as of model year 2001, has yet to return.

Sportsters

The superbike meanwhile went from strength to strength. In 1966 the XLCH got a new carburetor that gave more power and was something of a hazard in the home-maintenance department. But the semi-race model was the fastest thing on two wheels at mid-decade, which is what mattered to the buying public.

Meanwhile, the XLH improved with a new electric start added a year after the FLH's revision. Although kick starting can be mastered and impressive when it works,

Midway through the 1960s the XLCH peaked as a superbike, partly because it was the fastest motorcycle on the mass market, and partly because it looked as fast and fierce as it was.

The mid-1960s also marked the peak of the difference between the CH and the plain H Sportsters. This is a 1968 H equipped for touring. *Owner: Rick Newman*

having an engine that you know will start when you push a button is something to appreciate.

The XLCH era came with a hint of fashion. The factory's ads showed the bike with a high, right side single exhaust pipe routed around the magneto and carburetor. All the rival models had high pipes too, so off-road racers had much-needed ground clearance.

At the same time, the peanut fuel tank, with a capacity of only 2.25 gallons, meant taking to the open road required a constant search for open gas stations. The larger XLH tanks, three gallons and more, were more practical but nobody would use them. XLCH buyers bought two-up seats, but kept the small tank and opted for low, separate,

The XLH used the same frame and engine as the CH, but came with a larger fuel tank and headlight and longer rear fender, with optional luggage and windscreen. The chromed thingie outboard of the engine's vee is the horn, shaped and placed like that to balance the carburetor on the engine's other side. *Owner: Rick Newman*

Those are buckhorn bars, higher than those on the sporting CH, with speedometer and tachometer carried in a chromed housing and with idiot lights in a panel atop the forks. *Owner: Rick Newman*

drag pipes, because that's what the dirt track and drag racers used and that was the look of fashion.

The Lightweights

Good intentions don't always save the day. Harley-Davidson wasted no time supplementing its homemade two-strokes in their street, dirt, and dual-sport forms with new models from Aermacchi's Italian factory.

The new models were four-stroke singles, 250 cc and later 350 cc for some versions. The series began with the plain Sprint, echoing the XL story, which had full fenders and a big fuel tank. This was a practical urban bike with some merit on the open road.

Then came the Sprint H, with a really lovely fuel tank, sculpted in a teardrop shape and clearly done with Italian artistry. The Sprint H had a higher stage of tune, a high front fender, a skimpy rear fender, and a smaller taillight.

Cycle World tested early versions of both models and was impressed by the finish and the fun. Neither was a high-performance machine stock. The Sprint's top speed was 73 miles per hour, the Sprint H clocked 76 miles per hour. But they were entertaining and did the jobs they were supposed to do, and some successful racing bikes were based on the Sprints.

In model year 1963 Harley-Davidson advertised itself as the "world's widest choice," with seven motorcycles and one scooter. The Pacer and Scat were the two-strokes, both street legal, while the off-road Ranger had been dropped for lack of interest. Harley-Davidson was

In 1968 the XLH got an electric starter, with a bigger battery and the oil tank moved outboard. The ignition timer is below the carburetor and the starter motor is behind the ignition. The kick lever is gone. *Owner: Rick Newman*

in the golf cart business by then, but that wasn't seen as something that mattered to the motorcycle enthusiast.

Here begins the bad news. The scooter fad was fading. In 1965, the restricted Topper was dropped from the lineup and 500 of the (so to speak) full-performance Toppers sold. In 1966, Topper production ended. That same year the Pacer and Scat were joined by a similar motorcycle with fiberglass bodywork, an attempt to add style to dated machinery. The Bobcat, as it was called, lasted one year.

At the risk of getting ahead of the story, what happened to Harley-Davidson was a case of timing and fashion.

The timing part came because Harley-Davidson was in the off-road business before that business took flight. Few Americans had even heard of motocross, and people thought desert racing was for big men on big American or English twins.

A sizeable off-road market didn't happen until Bruce Brown, who popularized surfing with the film

CH instruments were separated, and the high beam light and toggle switch were the only controls. *Owner: Dave Carlton*

Endless Summer, released his movie *On Any Sunday.* When people saw Steve McQueen off-road riding that's what they wanted to do, especially because this happened just when Yamaha came out with the DT-1, a dirt bike you didn't need to overhaul every week.

Fashion went back to the family atmosphere mentioned earlier. The Harley-Davidson dealership was a club, with membership no less restricted because it wasn't written down.

The average Harley-Davidson dealer only wanted to deal with the average Harley-Davidson owner, not some kid shopping for a dinky two-stroke bike.

There were exceptions. Armando Magri in Sacramento, one of the best-selling agencies during this time, did well with the Hummers, 165s, and Scats. First, he says now, he was happy to have the customers, and second, he made sure they and their machines were taken care of.

The Sprints suffered from the social aspect, and were handicapped by their origin. In Europe in the 1960s, a 250 cc or 350 cc motorcycle was a man's machine and any potential owner knew his machine needed care, just as did owners of Italian and English cars of the period.

But in the United States, 250s were for kids, paperboy bikes as they said then, and kids are tough on equipment.

The Sprint H was sporting, modern, and as different from the Hummer or the FLH as it could be.

Competition

Before dealing with what seemed to be triumph (note lower case t; that isn't a pun) that became missed opportunity, one needs to look back to counter a false myth.

In the 1930s, the AMA recognized three classes of racing: Class A, professionals on racing engines with displacement the only limit; Class B, hill climbing with classes for overhead valve 45-cid engines and for production-based side-valve or pocket-valve engines; and Class C, ovals or road courses, amateurs only, using 45-cid (750 cc) or unlimited production engines.

Class C was for the sporting bike owner. The 45s were the main class because Harley and Indian offered sporting 45s and that's what most riders owned. The open class existed because the clubs wanted to attract the riders with the big machines.

And—this is the major fact in this lesson—motorcycles with overhead valve engines were permitted in the 45-ci class with a limit of 500 cc, or 30.50 ci, and if they were sold to the public.

Class C was supposed to keep costs down. It was open to owners who rode to the events, stripped the lights and so forth, raced, and rode home, just for the fun of it.

Among the causes of the Great Depression were the trade barriers various nations erected against each other's products. Countries made it tough on one another.

The United States had no import market. Only a few dealers offered English motorcycles. One dealer was a brave and resourceful man named Reg Pink. He had an agency in New York, where he sold a handful of English motorcycles of the sporting variety.

Motorcycling was a small world. Pink was an educated and aware guy. He knew that when England banned racing on public roads, back at the turn of the century, the Isle of Man invited the sporting gentry to race cars and motorcycles 'round their island. The racers used road machines on public roads, usually paved in 1907, and the

The H, like the 1964 model shown here, was the sporting version of the Sprint. With its high exhaust and front fender, huge and remote air cleaner, and grid of small bars to serve as a skid plate, the H could be used off road. *Owner: David Paryzek*

The Bobcat was a mix of new and old. Most visible here, in this 1966 trim, is the DKW-based two-stroke first built in the United States in 1947. Least visible is the swing-arm rear suspension with horizontal springs beneath the engine. A fiberglass shell covering the old-style frame and the fuel tank acts as a rear fender. *Owner: Tim Beitler*

venue was known as the Tourist Trophy, quickly shortened to the TT.

Pink also knew that the most important thing a dealer can offer is something his customers can do with their bikes. One day he borrowed some vacant land and laid out a course up and down hill, with turns left and right. He thought it mimicked the Isle of Man events, so he called it TT racing.

The motorcycle world was so small then that the AMA president dropped in on Pink one weekend and went to watch the TT. The racing seemed fun, so he got permission to send out the rules and requirements to all

the AMA clubs. TT caught on nationwide with the 750s and the big bikes and the name stuck.

This matters for the 1960s because racing virtually died during the Depression. Nobody could afford real race motorcycles.

The AMA took a bold step. They decided the national championship events could be contested on Class C machines without exotic engines or fuel. Lots of guys could race their daily drivers.

Class C was open to side-valve 750s because that's what the two native factories offered and what most of the AMA sportsmen rode. Pink and his customers were part of the

The luggage rack was standard equipment, but the bags were an option. The impression now is that the Bobcat's fiberglass body dictated its style and the curves designers could put into molds dictated its body shape. *Owner: Tim Beitler*

family, and because they rode ohv 500s, Class C allowed those engines as well, again subject to the requirement that they were road machines delivered equipped for highway use, and sold to anyone with the money or the credit.

This wasn't a handicap. It was an equivalency formula, as seen since racing began and still in use. Witness the world and national superbike classes, which allow 750 cc fours to compete against 1000 cc twins.

When Harley-Davidson designed the Sportster engine in the 1950s, they could have made an ohv 750, or they could have made an ohv 500.

But they saw Indian try to copy the English and go bust, literally and financially. They also knew that having more power is better than having equal power, so the XL engine began life with 54 cid. As seen earlier, it paid off.

The Bobcat's engine was bored and tuned but still outmoded by 1965. The frame was sturdy and conventional. The result was an adequate dual-sport bike lacking only in sales appeal.
Owner: Tim Beitler

Students of racing won't be surprised that serious competitors quickly stopped riding to the races, or that Harley-Davidson and Indian quickly began selling stripped and optioned versions of the road-going 750s.

In 1952, when Harley-Davidson introduced the somewhat modern (even though it retained a side-valve head) K, it came with the race version KR, sold to the public in dirt track or road race versions.

Then in 1957, Harley-Davidson replaced the side valve K with the ohv XL. Harley had a problem. They could lobby for a rule change, build a rule-bending ohv 500 single just for racing, or keep the old KR.

The dirt track KR was a production model at the same time it was a kit bike, an assembly of changeable parts. Notice the bolts below the seat and to the lower right of the primary cover. (Note also that this 1961 KR is fitted with a 1966 air cleaner.) *Owner: Pat Conroy*

They kept the old KR. At first thought this was a smart move. In 1960 the KR was a viable competitor. It had a foot shift, a hand clutch, like the English bikes, and it had more power to balance out the extra weight. The Harley tuners were a match for the BSA, Triumph, and Norton tuners.

The KRTT was the road race version. It came with a big fuel tank, a rear subframe to use with shock absorbers and a swing arm, and big drum brakes front and rear.

Cycle World tested a KRTT in 1963. With 30 pounds of fuel in the 6-gallon tank, the KRTT weighted 386 pounds, complete with an efficient fairing, which was permitted in road racing beginning with the 1963 season.

The KRTT had 48 bhp and topped out at 142 miles per hour in 1963. By the end of the model in 1969 and after 40 years of hard work and creative thinking, the KRTT would have 60 bhp and would average 150 miles per hour around the Daytona oval. Determination conquered the drawbacks.

We don't have similar facts about the KR, mostly because brakes were banned on dirt tracks until 1969 and none of the reporters back then had the skill (or maybe

This is a KRTT, same frame and engine as the KR, but with swing arm and shocks bolted to the main frame to provide rear suspension, along with kick-start and brakes shared with the street Sportster. This conversion worked for TT, dirt track with jumps, and road courses. *Owner: John Olsen*

the desire) to learn firsthand what she'd do. What matters here is that the KR weighed less, 300 pounds or so, had as much power, and won races.

The 1960s saw many rule changes. The original formula, Olympian in spirit and intent, allowed the privateer to have one machine, KR or not, and to swap parts. The KR frame and engine could be fitted with or without brakes, small or large fuel and oil tanks, rear suspension or rigid, bare or with fairing. All the parts were offered to the public and all Harley-Davidson dealers had the catalog and access to the factory's racing department.

The department in turn provided parts and advice for the racers.

Some got more help than others. Carroll Resweber won the national title in 1960 and 1961 on bikes tuned by Ralph Berndt, who worked at the Harley-Davidson plant but not for the racing department. Berndt liked doing things his own way and he liked even more beating the factory team, painting his bikes blue instead of the team's red, and even on one occasion forgetting to paint Harley-Davidson on the KR's tank. He got away with it because Walter Davidson, a

The KRTT needed wheel clearance, so the rear fender is a chopped (hint) Sportster part. The rear part of the seat is so the rider can slide into a racing crouch, not for a passenger. The foot peg has been moved back and the gear lever trails, rather than leads, so first gear is up and the next three are down. *Owner: John Olson*

The KR's magneto mounts at the front of the cases. This 1961 KRTT uses the production Linkert carburetor and giant air cleaner. The KR's alloy heads sport huge cooling fins. *Owner: John Olson*

cantankerous and enthusiastic fan, wanted to win more than he needed to be flattered.

The Olympian ideal extended to using that one machine in five events: short track, half mile, mile, TT, and road racing.

This changed early in the 1960s when most of the factories, domestic, English, and Japanese, had sturdy 250 cc singles. They became the mount for short track, first under Class A rules because they needed modifications to hold up under racing pressure, and then as Class C motorcycles when the rules changed to allow special frames and other equipment.

This was a time of entertaining chicanery when the rider was supposed to own his motorcycle despite the presence of factory teams and sponsored riders. Engine cases came from the factory with no numbers, for instance, or there would be three engines in the truck all numbered the same. Midway through the decade the AMA recognized the obvious and dropped the ownership rule.

The AMA as a whole wasn't exactly the one that did this. It was the work of its competition committee,

In 1963 the AMA allowed the use of fairings for road races. This is a 1963 KRTT, the side-valve KR engine fitted with suspension and brakes, with larger fuel and oil tanks, a skimpy, streamlined seat, and a fairing, all from the Harley-Davidson parts book. *Owner: Keith Campbell*

Ohio Harley dealer George Roeder, known as "The Flying Farmer" in his days on the pro circuit, backs his KR into a corner at a vintage race meet. The KR was an antique the day it was born, and a winner until the rules retired it.

comprised of men from the factories, tire companies and other suppliers, and other interested figures.

The idea was that the competing-but-interested parties would balance each other, and they did, generally voting their interest with an eye on the interests of the sport and the public.

Thus, the arrival of the Harley-Davidson Sprints, strong 250 cc singles, on par with the English 250s, allowed Walter Davidson to vote with his rivals for the switch to 250s for short track. There was also a lightweight road race class for production-based 250s.

Parked next to the KRTT at the *Cycle World* test was a CRTT. The CRTT used the road-version frame but was fitted with a full race engine, 28.5 bhp at 9,500, up from

18-bhp stock, and with a full fairing, big tank, and brakes. The test bike was fresh from a class win at Daytona and CW's editor was so instantly at home on the little rocket that he lost it in Riverside Raceway's esses, destroying the fairing but fortunately not himself in the process. "This is the first time we have dropped a test bike," the report said, "but it will probably not be the last."

The CRTT weighed 245 pounds topped off, and had a top speed of 116 miles per hour, which doesn't sound that fast but which obviously got the job done.

Next to the CRTT in the catalog were the CRS and the CR. The former was a Sprint stripped for action, as seen in scrambles, an early and rough form of motocross, and in desert races.

The CR was the short track Sprint, and it was mostly a kit. The CRS engine was bolted into a special frame, which put the weight low and in the balance needed to keep the bike in a constant left slide. The frames came from aftermarket makers, Track Master or Champion usually, but to keep the spirit of the rules, Harley-Davidson dealers were informed of the parts and options and the private racer could get what they needed through the dealership, as was intended when the rules were written in 1934.

Generally, the racing was fair and it was close. Resweber won the number one plate in 1960 and 1961. Dick Mann took it for Triumph and Matchless in 1963. The title went back to Harley the next three seasons with Roger Reiman and Bart Markel. Then Gary Nixon

Short track rules during the 1960s allowed production engines in racing frames, so this 1968 CR was built from parts ordered through the dealership. The CR was brakeless, with 19-inch wheels front and back. That's an accessory seat and the now-legendary peanut fuel tank. *Owner: Dave Georgianni*

Triumphed in 1967 and 1968. Mert Lawwill (see *On Any Sunday,* what I consider to be the best motorcycle movie ever) won in 1969, followed by Gene Romero, another Triumph, in 1970.

This is presented here in such detail because the mark of an intellectual in any country is disdain for his native culture. American college guys and the press back then heavily favored English motorcycles. Imagine their shock when they went to motorcycling mecca and learned the English intellectuals worshipped Italian motorcycles.

Because of this disdain, or maybe just because Harley-Davidson was the overdog, the press and some fans complained that Harley had an advantage, as if The Motor Company had told the AMA to handicap the English. As the records show, that did not happen.

In a sense, though, some of those handicaps worked against Harley-Davidson in the long run.

By 1960 the Olympian notion of racing what you rode was history. A KR or KRTT or CRS was a specialized motorcycle that could be bought only by those who knew

The post-1966 racing Sprints got an engine with shorter stroke, bigger bore and improved internals, raising the power to 35 bhp. Compare the head and barrel here with the engine in the earlier, road-going Sprints. This bike wears No. 87 in tribute to Mark Brelsford. *Owner: Dave Georgianni*

who to ask for what. While Harley-Davidson raced production motorcycles, in a strictly legal sense, the English produced racing motorcycles. That's the lead the Japanese followed. You could buy a BSA Gold Star or a Suzuki X-6 and actually race it after doing some basic preparation. You couldn't buy a race bike from your Harley dealer.

This meant first that the grassroots guys, who kind of thought racing would be fun to try, didn't try it on Harleys.

Next, while Harley-Davidson had at least a fair share of the win ads, they never actually told the reader anything about the winning KRTT, simply because it was an exotic and archaic piece of equipment with only the bare outline and configuration of any Harley on the showroom floor.

This wasn't a mistake. It was a set of circumstances into which Harley-Davidson's management had been pushed by other circumstances. But it did mean that piles of money were being spent on racing for not a lot of return, short or long term.

Speaking of circumstances, the English found themselves in a bit of a pinch when the 500-cc ohv engines were no longer the hot setup by the time the mid-1960s

Mark Brelsford, national No. 87 rode a machine just like this to the AMA title in 1972. Brelsford takes time from his trucking business and demonstrates his old short-tracker at a vintage meet. *Owner: Dave Georgianni*

arrived. The English countered the Harley 883-cc XLCH with 650-cc and 750-cc twins, so they weren't racing their hottest models either.

And they had gained power within the AMA. So in 1968 the competition committee voted to revise the rules. The changes were to be done in stages, with production 750-cc engines—no limit on valve design or number of cylinders—allowed on the dirt tracks for 1969 and road courses in 1970.

The KRs went into the history books in a blaze of glory.

Cal Rayborn was one of the best road racers of his—and perhaps any—era. He won the Daytona 200 in 1968 on a KRTT, done for the first time in the now-mandatory orange, black, and white livery, using a two-carburetor engine cranked to 58 bhp, fitted to a frame that wrapped around the engine.

In 1969, the last year of the old formula, the KRTTs looked the same but weren't as fast and nobody knew why.

Aermacchi followed Harley's code, so the 250 cc road racer was designated the CRTT because it had brakes and suspension. The small machines that raced with small fairings shared engines with the dirt racers.

Road racers, here a 1964 CRTT, used massive drum brakes long after cars had gone to discs. Like the dirt models, the CRTT benefited from aftermarket tanks, seats, and such, listed in the catalog. *Owner: Mike Mahan*

Then it rained and the race was postponed for a week. Team manager Dick O'Brien and his guys found the problem, and Rayborn won again.

The first dirt race of 1969, featuring the ohv 750 English bikes against the poor old side-valve KR, was even more dramatic. Defending AMA champion Gary Nixon showed up with a Triumph triple and a Triumph twin. He tested both, picked the lighter twin, and lost the main event to Fred Nix on a Harley team KR.

The press couldn't believe it. "What happened?" they badgered Nixon.

The champ was fierce but fair.

"I got beat," he snapped. "That's what happened."

The Sell-Out

Pause here to reflect on sportsmanship and then to wonder: if Harley-Davidson's reputation for value and engineering began when Walter Davidson won a major enduro in 1908, and if the factory had fielded a works team since 1914, and if factory guys were on the AMA's competition committee, why was Harley-Davidson fielding a 1929 engine against 1969 competition?

The answer was money, as in research and development funds, and timing. The founding fathers had been replaced by a generation responsible to stockholders. The new leaders couldn't afford to gamble.

Philosopher George Santayana wrote: "Those who cannot remember the past are condemned to repeat it."

That may be so, but it also may be true that those who pay too much attention to the past risk being run over when the future rolls in.

The managers and owners at The Motor Company in the early 1960s were intelligent, experienced men. They knew their field and their market. As noted earlier, they were open to new ideas, invented in house or not. There was a constant program of potential models, including an overhead-cam V-twin with the vee at 60 degrees. But the managers knew what worked and what didn't and they read the obituaries of companies such as Indian that had gone too far too fast.

Harley-Davidson had made what the record should show was the right moves.

At the same time, Harley's owners, along with the owners and managers of the English, Italian, German, and Spanish motorcycle companies, seriously underestimated the size and strength of the opposition.

Some figures back that assessment. In 1950, Harley-Davidson had 60 percent of the American motorcycle market, which included about 40,000 units annually.

By 1965, the American motorcycle market had grown to more than 200,000 units per model year. Harley's share was six percent. Yes, six percent, despite the new Electra Glide pushing big twin sales to their best since the near-monopoly days of 1951.

In 1959, Harley-Davidson's retail sales totaled $16 million, while newcomer Honda's U.S. sales came to $500,000.

Pure racing parts such as the fiberglass fuel tank and clip-on bars, short stubs clamped to the fork tubes, let the rider tuck behind the fairing. *Owner: Mike Mahan*

The ERS was a compromise, in that the 250-cc four-strokes couldn't compete with the two-strokes, so Harley-Davidson/Aermacchi came up with a 350-cc engine. It has the backbone frame tube with a network of smaller tubing, but shares brakes and teardrop fuel tank with the Sprint H. *Owner: Jim Oldiges*

The ERS had a left-side kick-start, right side shifting. The tachometer drive is off the center of the gearcase cover, and the arm above it and to the right activates the clutch. The odd barrier below the teardrop tank is a shield for the float bowl and air intake. *Owner: Jim Oldiges*

The late KRTT was modern in every way except the engine. It had a large efficient fairing, massive drum front brake, light disc rear brake, and full suspension. The KRTT introduced the orange-and-black factory color scheme and won the Daytona 200 in 1968 and 1969. *Owner: Walt Schaefer*

By 1965, Harley-Davidson's sales had grown to $29.6 million. Honda's total was $77 million.

As film producer Samuel Goldwyn said, if people don't want to go to the movies, you can't stop them.

The top men at Harley-Davidson knew the motorcycle market was going to continue growing. They knew they needed new, different, and improved motorcycles and they'd done all they could do with what they had.

But many more people wanted motorcycles than any student of history would have predicted, and they wanted Hondas nearly three times as much as they wanted Harleys.

The owning families thought seriously about this. Then they made a fateful decision. Up to this point, Harley-Davidson had kept ownership and financed expansion through loans. Now they believed they couldn't get enough investment and expansion capital that way so they decided to take The Motor Company public.

During the 1990s people became more familiar with the term initial public offering (IPO) and the frenzy it could generate. Everybody seemed to be in the market. It was as if, to invent an illustration, a bunch of financial wizards went public with goldengoose.com and people went wild even though no one saw any golden eggs or even a goose (investors excepted).

But in the 1960s the public wasn't in the market. The term *stock market* brought back memories of 1929's Black Friday.

Those in the market were cautious. They were investors and they expected a return on their investments.

Here's a bobber/chopper from the early 1960s. It is a side-valve VL, with a rigid rear frame, cut rear fender, no front fender or front brake, high bars, leading-link forks, a pad behind the seat, and a push bar, predating the sissy bar to come. Mile racers used skinny front wheels, such as this one. The cat's-eye taillight and license plate are mounted on the side so they don't spoil the view. *Cycle World*

They expected to receive golden eggs, quaintly called dividends. And they expected the company to take care of the goose from which the eggs came.

This era matters because then there was no frenzy. Several hundred stockholders wanted the 1965 IPO. Harley-Davidson historian Harry Sucher says financial reports claimed it was more like a few thousand.

Either way, the founding families had bought or retained enough stock in the corporation to retain control, while the other stockholders were standard, conventional investors or Harley-Davidson employees or long-time dealers.

This was the low point for the Harley-Davidson Motor Company, lower than when the car overtook the motorcycle as cheap transportation, when the founders cut their own salaries during the Depression, and when (as this reporter hopes to establish) Harley-Davidson was part of a conglomerate. Turning the family corporation into a publicly traded company was supposed to save The Motor Company, but the fix didn't work.

Jumping a little ahead of the story, historian Sucher says he was told that the top man at American Machine and Foundry (AMF) was critical of the decisions made by Harley-Davidson executives during this time period.

That sounds like hindsight.

The Motor Company made some attempts to become more profitable. The M-60, a two-stroke moped meant to replace the scooter, sold but not well enough.

Next, the dragbike look. The Sportster engine was stronger than the larger F-series 74, and could be bored and stroked, so the XL engine was the basis for almost all Harley-Davidson dragbikes. This is a 1957 engine in a custom frame that moves the engine forward and down. The rigid rear suspension, kicked-out forks, and the tiny seat are all features we'll see again. *Owner: Tony Daya*

Ditto the Rapido, a 125 cc dirt bike that wasn't a match for the Japanese models.

The rest of the motorcycle industry made similar attempts. The English, in particular Norton, offered electric-start middleweight twins aimed at the Japanese bikes. Triumph and BSA came out with what they must have believed to be the largest and most powerful motorcycles the human body could control, sporting 750 cc triples, which at least matched Harley's XLCH.

To no avail, the established companies followed the business practices they had always followed. They produced a year's worth of frames, for instance, all at once and they paid suppliers and workers and built storage space. They considered all those parts assets.

Honda and the other newcomers, though, didn't see it that way. They had no traditional industrial habits. The new guys didn't want to spend company money on, say, a tire, until the man lacing up the wheel reached behind him for one. They didn't want to buy components until the assembly of components was sold.

The old firms didn't yet know what would hit them, even when they knew they were in trouble.

As something of a parallel threat, the stakeholders in the newly public Harley-Davidson believed with some justification that they were entitled to a return on their investment.

During this time, the late 1960s, Harley-Davidson sales held up so The Motor Company paid regular dividends. But sales weren't keeping up with the market.

Back with racing's microcosm, when the revised AMA began casting about for a new set of rules, the engineers in the racing department knew what was going to happen. But they could not get the money to do what

needed to be done, so they too settled for doing what they could and adapting parts already in existence.

None of it worked. Late in 1967 the owners and managers of Harley-Davidson decided the company might not survive without major outside investment, and that the only way to get that was to be bought by a larger corporation.

The Chopper Phenomenon

Meanwhile, equal to Harley-Davidson's financial woes and the astonishing growth of the motorcycle market, another sort of history was being made, a chunk of history credited for a major share of The Motor Company's survival and salvation.

Like most history, it begins before anyone paid attention.

As mentioned earlier, we as a species don't take good notes. No historian has established exactly why we call soldiers "GIs," or from where the name of the Jeep came. Pioneer hot rodder Dean Batchelor, who was there at the beginning and later wrote the definitive history of that sport, said he was unable to pin down exactly where the term *hot rod* came from, or where it first was used.

The dragbike look went to the street. This is another 1957 XL engine, but in a chopper-style frame with a gooseneck, as they called it back in the day, forming the steering head. These were individual machines—witness the front brake combined with drag bars and an enduro taillight. But the look, the stretched front and muscular haunches, were what you saw if you checked street fashion.

With that in mind, we do know that back in the late 1910s and early 1920s, when other gearheads were putting sporty bodies and speed equipment on Model T Fords, some motorcycle nuts began adding and subtracting racing equipment borrowed from the board track or road-race machines. The modified motorcycles were usually lower, lighter, and louder than stock and the popular term of the day was *cut-downs*.

When the Depression-inspired Class C rules opened racing to amateurs on stock bikes, and when TT racing took the big machines off road, a series of options and modifications improved handling and performance.

Enduro classes and hill climb classes began for big bikes, and governing bodies allowed changes from stock. Kits raised the engine in the frame, exhaust pipes became higher to accommodate logs and rocks, and front suspensions were extended for extra clearance. Handlebars became higher, so the rider could stand up on the jumps. Dirt track machines sometimes had push bars, upright tubing aft of the seat, for better push-starts. One speed trick was to use a 21-inch front wheel on the mile, for less friction and rolling resistance, and the wider 19-inch wheel on the half mile because it gripped better. Short races meant a smaller, lighter fuel tank. A shorter, lighter, flared front fender replaced the full-length, valenced rear fender. The front wheel ran exposed.

A mild form of these changes appeared in the 1930s. In the 1940s, after the war, surplus motorcycles flooded the market. The modified motorcycle became more popular and picked up the name "bobber" or "bob-job." Just as girls in the 1920s shortened or bobbed their hair, riders bobbed their bikes.

Drag racing, as a formal and recognized sport rather than what the law calls an "unauthorized contest of speed," appeared officially in 1951. Drag racers, like hill climbers, stretched the wheelbase and extended the front ends for better weight transfer.

All the above is documented.

Harder to pin down is the precise time and place the modified motorcycle evolved from bobber to chopper.

In the early 1960s the purpose of modifications went from performance to style. All the elements—the long wheelbase, high bars and pipes, small tank, marginal lights and muffling, high and skinny front wheels and wide, fat rear wheels, and even the outrageous paint—can be traced from chopper back to bobber, TT bike, hill climb bike, and drag strip bike.

The major difference was that when you take all the changes designed to improve an element of performance, as in ground clearance, weight transfer, and stability at speed, and mix them into one package you have a motorcycle whose function is impaired by its form.

Choppers, as awkward and uncomfortable as they are unstable, became an art form to some degree because they are terrible motorcycles. Women laced into corsets, and men buttoned into high collars could take lessons from the chopper crowd.

The only visible sign of the chopper craze in the official record was that the AMA enacted a limit on the height of the handlebars in competition.

Turning old motorcycles into rolling displays became a hobby and then a business. Chopper magazines sprang up, to some degree because the standard magazines wanted nothing to do with motorcycles intended to be shown, not ridden.

Significant pause here. Most choppers started as old Harley-Davidsons. There was no magic about it. Choppers were built from used parts. Harley-Davidson had ruled the U.S. market for years, so more organ-donor Harleys waited in the back of barns than any other brand.

Meanwhile a culture clash came along. For generations the sport's backbone had been the old-line dealership and the club that rode in unison and uniform. Since the early 1900s a rough and rowdy element started, leading to organized clubs creating what amounted to dress codes and contests for best-dressed bike, clubs, and individual riders.

Riders who put time and money into buying new motorcycles and adding all manners of extras had no use for those who revived old machines and chopped stuff off.

That attitude worked both ways.

Expectations Are Resolved

AMF ENSURES SURVIVAL

Contrary to folk wisdom, what looks right doesn't always work right. This is a 1970 XR-750. It looks as right as any motorcycle ever made, but it blew up on a regular basis. As an extra icon, AMF introduced that wonderful red, white, and blue No. 1. *Owner: Frank Vespa, Classic Cycles*

ob Hansen began racing back in the days of the Indian Scout, then switched to Matchless. Eventually he persuaded Mr. Honda to build a 750 cc Four and prepared the Honda that won the Daytona 200 and put Big Red into racing history. Hansen then did the same for Kawasaki.

He knows motorcycling and its history.

Hansen was on the AMA committee during the battle to revise Class C. He recalled the meeting during which Walter Davidson, never one to let polite language interfere with freedom of expression, exploded: "If you blankety-blank so-an-sos are so rippety-doodle in favor of dippy-donut 750s, then by tarnation you can have the expletive deleted things!"

Ha ha, chortled one of the English proponents, guess we showed him.

Well, Hansen said at the time, sometimes getting Harley-Davidson all worked up isn't such a good idea.

The first XR had a fiberglass fuel tank and fender/seat styled by the Wixom brothers, a top grade steel frame based on the successful KTRTT Lowboy frame, and an XLR-based engine de-stroked from 883 cc to 747 cc. *Owner Frank Vespa, Classic Cycles*

The cast iron heads and cylinders worked on the road-going XL engines, and for the XLR, which raced TT and got to slow down. But the '70 XR had to run wide open on the miles and road courses and melted because it couldn't shed heat fast enough. The magneto is mounted up front where the XL carried its generator. *Owner: Frank Vespa, Classic Cycles*

Hansen was right and the English brand whose fan gloated that day was dumped into the trashcan of history. And we all know what became of the company Indian called Hardly-Stumblehome.

How this happy ending came from the depths of lagging product and unimaginative management begins with some business history.

Even big business is subject to the whim of fashion. In the 1960s the fashion in business was diversity, with conglomerates buying up any and all smaller firms with which they could have any common ground.

When Harley-Davidson's board of directors voted to look for a bigger corporation to keep them afloat, up stepped AMF, which made recreational products such as bicycles and bowling equipment and heavy industrial machinery, and Bangor Punta, a conglomerate with all manners of operations including the Waukesha Engine Co. of Milwaukee.

Lengthy and complicated battles in court and in the press led to Harley-Davidson stock being valued beyond expectations, and to AMF owning Harley-Davidson.

Of course the announcements said nothing would change. Of course the changes were many.

The roadrace XRTT had an even larger inheritance. On the left is a 1972 XRTT, with the alloy-topped two-carb engine shared with the dirt model, but with the big fairing and tanks done by the Wixoms in 1968, and with the Lowboy frame and suspension, plus big disc brakes front and rear. On the right, the last KRTT, with the old side valve 750 engine in the Lowboy frame, the Wixom bodywork and four-shoe drum front brake. *Owners: John and Mary Schultz, Rusty Lowry*

This led—and we are condensing some intricate struggles here—to the current myth that AMF was greedy, arrogant, and careless, and that AMF did Harley-Davidson a great deal of harm.

Not true. The first counterattack involves common sense: Why would AMF spend millions of dollars acquiring a company to harm that company?

The more logical reasoning is that AMF acted like the giant corporation it was. AMF's managers preferred spending money on the plant first, the product second, and the people third.

Harley-Davidson's original factory in Milwaukee was upgraded, another even better plant was acquired, and AMF transferred most of the actual production to still another facility, in York, Pennsylvania.

Good business sense, or good financial sense, the travel and transfers did not make life easier. The new executives didn't understand the all-in-the-family atmosphere of the old firm. The workers, who were part of a union-oriented work force anyway, weren't happy and most of the members of the founding families found themselves on the outside. Whether they jumped by choice or were pushed out is still debatable.

Another distressing factor is that in the late 1960s and early 1970s the federal government took more control of vehicle design, as in the Safety Act of 1966. Car and motorcycle makers found themselves coping with emissions and crash requirements and the products suffered. Parts falling off or failing plagued many models.

Although it is true that the Harley-Davidsons of that period did have more problems than they should have had, it wasn't because AMF meant for customers to have to walk home.

Harley's motocross team used the state-of-the-art two-stroke made by Aermacchi, and hired some good riders, but did not have the budget to compete with Japan's big four. The production MXers did not sell well enough to justify the program. *Owner: John Steel*

The good side of AMF owning Harley was improved production capabilities. When the managers bought Harley-Davidson back from AMF, they had the factories and the equipment they needed to make the product better. But that came after Harley survived tough years.

The first place to look and the best place to prove that Bob Hansen was right when he said you don't always want to poke Harley-Davidson with a stick, is Harley's racing department.

When the British changed the rules in 1968, all the Harley-Davidson racing department could do was rework the XLR to have a shorter stroke and a new frame. They announced the model, the XR-750, for the 1969 season. The production models, made in a batch of 200, weren't seen in public until the opening of the 1970 season.

The model was a mitigated disaster because the iron-topped XR engine overheated and blew up time and again. The 1970 AMA Grand National title went to Triumph rider Gene Romero.

The batwing fairing must have surprised even The Motor Company. It wasn't the first fairing, and it didn't provide full protection, but it was larger and more effective than a windshield. *Owner: Gary Walker*

The early XR-750 was mitigated because by 1970 AMF provided a budget for serious research and development. Team manager Dick O'Brien and engineer Peter Zylstra came up with an alloy-topped engine with a shorter stroke, larger bore, and more power. It was an engine that lasted an entire race.

The new XR-750 was introduced in 1972 and won instantly. Yamaha took the GN title a couple of times during the 1970s, Honda did the same (with the XR-750 Harley would have built if Harley-Davidson had Honda's money) during the 1980s. Yamaha quit losers, Honda quit winners and if anything in racing is sure, it is that someone riding an XR-750 will win the AMA title in 2001.

Moral: Don't mess with Harley-Davidson.

To complete the record here, AMF extended the Harley-Davidson effort in small and beginner bikes, switching to Aermacchi-made two-strokes when the Japanese makers proved that was the way to go. But the

Because the fairing and bags were options, and because buyers liked to display their extras, the color of the fairing and bags often didn't match the rest of the machine. *Owner: Jim Glasner*

Europeans couldn't offer equal value for money and the plug was pulled on the tiddlers in 1978. Meanwhile, though, the motocross 250 cc engines gave the Harley team competitive power for national short track racing.

The Big Twins

Continued development of the big twins was at least half the power behind Harley-Davidson's survival.

In model year 1969 when things were not going at all well anywhere else in the company, the touring market got a new flagship.

The name was the same, FLH, and the model was the King of the Highway, but the top-of-the-line 1969 model had a distinctive full fairing mounted on the handlebars and fiberglass boxes, saddlebags as we still call them, bracketing the rear wheel.

No one took much note at the time, and the actual machine didn't change much. Aside from protecting the riders better, the fairings allowed longer days in the saddle.

That's what people wanted. The FLH remained Harley's bestseller, even if the rivals pulled away in total sales. Naturally the company kept improving the model. In 1970 an alternator replaced the sometimes-fragile generator, leading to the nickname "Cone Shovel" instead of what was earlier called the "Generator Shovel."

Then came a different kind of inspiration, the 1971 FX Superglide. Frame, engine and tanks are FLH, the front end comes from the Sportster, and the fiberglass seat/fender was a 1970 XL option. Like the Captain America bike used in the film *Easy Rider*, the Superglide was a collection of used parts. Owner: Benjy Steele

But there was more to it than that. Fitted with what became known as the Batwing fairing, the appeal of the FLH surpassed function. The interstate highway system had opened the road. The fully fitted FLH was the touring motorcycle of choice and its profile became part of every American's memory. If you made flash cards, the side view of that big Harley, two people sitting upright behind that unique fairing, would be the image several generations have of the motorcycle.

Not convinced? When Harley-Davidson later introduced the FLT, which featured a frame-mount fairing that worked even better than the batwing, they had to revise the model to carry the old batwing version because buyers demanded it.

And when the rivals 30 years later shoved their way into the retro-style touring market, they used batwing-style fairings.

The Future Arrives on a Superglide

The final myth to challenge is that the outlaws, the scruffy bad guys, loyally saved Harley-Davidson when the company was at its worst.

Not so. Even the part they did play was just that: a part in a play.

On this subject, the actual decade fits nicely. An informal survey of Harley-Davidson dealers in 1960 through 1970 shows that the customer base became better educated and had higher incomes than expected.

The outlaws, the club members know as "one percenters" because that was the AMA's estimate of their share of the motorcycling public, were there.

"My rule was no colors (club jackets) in the shop and they honored it," recalls Armando Magri, who owned the Harley-Davidson dealership in Sacramento,

The Captain America paint wasn't an exact copy, but it did repeat the theme. *Owner: Benjy Steele*

California. "They'd drape their jackets over their bikes before they came in."

Former San Diego dealer Brad Andres didn't need to make rules. "They were polite, they paid cash, and they didn't haggle."

Rather than outlaws, Ray Texter of Lancaster, Pennsylvania, remembers when the clientele changed from the military man to the professional man.

As for differences among riders, Andres notes a gulf between those who bought twins, and those who bought singles.

"Sell a big bike and he'd ride out and you'd never see him again. The little bike buyers were always fussing about something."

What mattered more at the end of the 1960s was image, not reality, even though the bad element—the brawlers, drinkers, and hooligans—never totaled more than a few thousand men nationwide.

But movie studios cashed in with at least a score of class B movies featuring hard men, loose women, and big Harley-Davidsons. The chopper image became powerful, even though few one-percenters were on the road. Here's a little-known fact: before the chopper fad swept the movies, Peter Fonda rode a BMW. Honest.

The man of this hour was William G. Davidson, grandson of the founding William Davidson, head of Harley-Davidson's styling department and one of the family members who stuck it out through the AMF years.

Willie G., as he's known, had the idea of an optional seat and fender, supplied by the companies fiberglass division, on the 1970 Sportster. It wasn't a hit.

Even so, Willie G. watched the street. He knew choppers and drag racing were selling movies and magazines and that private owners were bobbing, chopping, and stripping their machines. He took an FLH frame, engine, and rear suspension and attached Sportster front forks, wheel, and headlight. The tractor-style FLH seat was replaced with the fiberglass unit from the Sportster. The electric start and big battery were removed.

The completed machine, strikingly different from any Harley yet, was a less-extreme chopper, displayed without emblems. Motorcycle fans at shows, races, and rallies liked what they saw.

In 1971 Harley-Davidson introduced the experiment as a production model, coded FX, F for the big twin engine and frame, X for the Sportster front end and fiberglass. It was named the Superglide, one word no hyphen.

It was a hit. The writers at motorcycle magazines were baffled. The Superglide wasn't as sporting as the XL or as comfortable as the FLH, and it lacked convenience. Function had been sublimated to form. What sort of motorcycle was that?

A popular one. Willie G. had intuited or deduced that the biking public was seduced by the movies. He knew that Harley buyers could afford what they wanted and that they would buy a machine that looked as if they'd done it themselves, an appeal all the stronger to those who didn't have the mechanical skills needed to perform such modifications.

The Superglide sold strongly at first. The next move was to replace the fiberglass seat with one more conventional, something many buyers did anyway, swap the FLH fuel tanks for the lovely teardrop tank first seen on the Sprint H, and replace the electric start. The FXE sold even better than the FX, proving that when you get the form right, you can improve the function.

The Superglide went from strength to strength. The model became two models, then a full model line, each time getting closer and closer to the kicked-out, laid-back chopper image.

The Superglide became known as the "Nighttrain," inspired by a song, and had blue (or black, or even maroon) paint as an option. The fiberglass seat was as comfortable as it looks.

Sportsters

There must be some wisdom in the saying "If you don't move forward, you move back." For the Sportster, that came in the late 1960s.

The XL wasn't alone. All the classic big twins from Triumph, Norton, and BSA were eased into the shadows by smaller two-stroke twins from Suzuki and Yamaha, then by two-stroke triples from Kawasaki and finally by the 750-cc and 900-cc fours from Honda and Kawasaki.

Harley-Davidson Sportsters countered with improvements, some real, some imagined. In 1968 the XLH gained an electric start, and the touring version acquired a windshield, larger fuel tank, fiberglass bags, a tiny sissy bar to keep the passenger in place, and extra chrome, recreating the miniature FLH the factory had in mind for the XL back in 1957.

Next, more or less in order, the XLCH magneto was replaced by the XLH's points and coil, the dry clutch gave way to a wet clutch, which was more durable at the expense of a heavier pull, and the XLCH got an electric start, making the two models nearly identical except for fuel tank size. Finally, in 1972, the XL's bore was increased from 3 inches to 3.18 inches, which raised displacement from 883 to a rounded-off 1000 cc.

By 1971 the XLCH had a battery ignition and starter, but it kept the light and compact style of the more sporting early versions. *Ron Hussey*

In 1972 the XL engine got a larger bore and displacement increased to a rounded-off 1000 cc. The Sportster retained its 1000cc displacement until the Iron Head XL engine was replaced by the Evolution powerplant in 1986. *Ron Hussey*

None of these changes were radical. In fact, the Sportster was in something of a holding pattern.

Singles and Servi-cars

Surely because the new owners and executives as well as the old hands under new control had plenty on their plates, the holding pattern for the middleweight twins carried over with the other lines.

As mentioned, when the four-stroke singles couldn't compete, Harley-Davidson tried a line of Italian-made two-strokes. They didn't win on Sunday and they didn't sell on Monday. In 1978 the effort could no longer be justified and the line was dropped. The Italian connection was sold and transformed, minus the Harley-Davidson or AMF names. It became Cagiva.

The three-wheeled Servi-car continued until 1973, presumably because enough true service stations and dealerships still used them.

The Era Ends

When the 1960s officially began, Harley-Davidson was a private company owned by its founding families. It also was the biggest fish in a small and specialized pond.

The families had been bought out or had sold out by the time the 1970s started. Harley sales had increased, but the new competitors had eclipsed all the old totals and taken nearly all the larger market. Worse yet, the competition offered better value, the very virtue that kept The Motor Company in business in the early years when more than a hundred early rivals failed or faded away.

Then things got worse. AMF decided total sales were the key to profit, so production was ramped up. The push of supply replaced the pull of demand. Harley dealers, who always told the factory how many bikes to send, resented being told how many they had to accept, finance, and sell. Some signed on with the new makes. If it were true that the Japanese factories also pressured the dealers to sell, sell, sell, it was equally true that the Hondas and Yamahas were, well, better machines.

The lowest of several low points came in 1974 when workers went on strike for 101 days.

Quality was down and even the media who liked Harley-Davidson, a minority viewpoint at the time, struggled to find ways to defend the brand without lying to readers.

A Happy Ending

THE EAGLE SOARS

In 1994 the sinking feeling caused by seeing this shape in a mirror was the same feeling our fathers and grandfathers had in 1964.
Owner: Connecticut State Police

arley-Davidson recovered, but not everyone lived happily ever after. Some of the old people and some of the new people did a wonderful job playing the cards dealt them in the 1960s and even earlier.

In 1949 the president of Indian Motorcycles decided Americans were ready for motorcycling. Indian offered new models, but went out of business. Honda Motor Co. attempted the same in 1959 and became an industry leader.

Timing is everything.

Although it sounds odd, Honda must be considered a factor in Harley-Davidson's success because Honda enlarged the pie. The motorcycle market multiplied during the 1960s. The Motor Company didn't hang on to its large share of a smaller market, but sales did go up and the Harley buyer profile became more upscale.

In 1969 Hollywood gave us *Easy Rider,* which introduced choppers to the mainstream. That same year *On Any Sunday* supplied an honest portrayal of courage, skill, and camaraderie, and introduced dirt bikes to the public.

In 2000, the curator of the Otis Chandler Museum of Transportation and Wildlife, Oxnard, California, added a replica of the Captain America chopper. You know the bike? Of course you do. The curator was amazed that the movie bike was the best-known machine in the place. Everybody who walked in the door walked up to the red-white-and-blue Panhead. Even kids knew the bike.

With the 1990s came a motorcycle boom. Harley-Davidson was the chief beneficiary and reclaimed the major share of the big bike market. Some of the buyers owned a Harley-Davidson because it was the cool thing to do. Others were people who had always wanted to ride motorcycles, but waited until it was in fashion. The leaders of the new pack were those who began years earlier.

As for dirt bikes, finding an American male rider who didn't learn to ride a dirt bike in his teens is a nearly impossible feat.

The parallel good move in 1980 was the FLT, which introduced the frame-mount fairing and the isolation mounts for the drivetrain. The FLT was big and came with every available touring accessory. *Owner: Benjy Steele*

A new entry-level Harley, introduced when every dollar counted, was the XLX, a Sportster with no chrome, solo seat, black paint, and a price of $3,995. The sales pitch worked. *Ron Hussey*

Rewind now to 1972, when AMF controlled Harley-Davidson with the Superglide, Sportster, XR-750, and FLH in position. The Motor Company survived the strike, and the arrival of federal rules and regulations. In 1977, AMF executive Vaughn Beals became Harley-Davidson's president, AMF opened the Rodney Gott Museum in York, and a disappointed Harley buyer founded the Harley-Davidson Owner's Association.

In 1978, the Aermacchi factory was closed, and then sold.

In 1980, Beals moved up and Charley Thompson became president of Harley-Davidson. He introduced quality control and increased employee pride.

That same year saw the arrival of the FLT, the big, new touring bike. It had a larger engine mounted in isolators, so

the drive train's inherent vibrations didn't reach the riders. The nickname was "Rubber Glide," but the mounts weren't made of rubber. Then came the FXB Sturgis, the B representing a drive belt.

In 1981, Beals and Thompson, Willie and John Davidson, and several other Harley-Davidson, AMF, and family members hocked what they could, borrowed the rest from banks, and bought Harley-Davidson from AMF.

Their slogan, "The Eagle Soars Alone," said more than it should have, as time told.

In 1982, President Ronald Reagan imposed increased tariffs on the big Japanese models, while Harley plants got the just-in-time system used in Japan. Some workers were laid off as productivity increased and Harley-Davidson introduced the FXR Superglide, a sporting model using the isolation mounts first seen on the FLT.

In 1983 the factory founded the Harley Owners Group, and the nonfactory group faded away. The next year Evolution engines began to replace the Shovelhead big twins and XLs.

By 1986 Harley-Davidson was in the black and the owners went public. Again, timing was everything and the offering was snapped up. Since then Harley-Davidson has seen record sales, new plants, and a world-class success story.

Roll the Credits

None of the above success came nearly as easily as it looks now, so when it comes to taking bows and accepting the bouquets, we must recap a bit.

The expanded market, the use of bikers as heroes and villains in the movies, and the revised public image, good and bad (they both attract fans), were not incidental. Those cast members deserve a curtain call.

Next, being a Harley fan was easy when only two marques, Harley and Indian, existed. Owning a twin cam- or Evo-powered motorcycle that will run with no tools on board isn't hard now either. Between those, though, came a choice of newer, faster, more reliable—heck, make that better—bikes. That's when The Motor Company knew who its friends were.

So, the "bad guys" weren't the ones who saved Harley-Davidson.

The numbers back that. Harley-Davidson sales were 20,000 to 30,000 units annually during the bad times. Those sales are too high to be only the one percenters.

By 1984, when Harley introduced the Softail, chopper styling had moved mainstream. The Softail recreated the classic hardtail lines by connecting a triangulated swingarm to a rear suspension that was hidden underneath the engine. The 2000 Softail Deuce, with its bobbed fenders and extended tank, took chopper styling to an even higher level.

The customer (and fashion) wins, as the bar-mounted batwing fairing became available on the FLT platform. The modern Electra Glide still presents the same profile in the new millennium as the FLH presented in 1969.

What does add up is the buyer who came aboard in the 1960s. That buyer could afford a new machine every few years, joined an AMA club, and took his wife on tour. What also adds up is the importance of the old-time dealer, who was his own chief mechanic and prided himself on having the parts before the customer knew he needed them.

The money and engineering to make a winner out of the XR-750, to introduce the full-dress touring bike, and to gamble on the Superglide, came from AMF. So did the new plants and the enlarged advertising budget.

When the eagle soared alone, the new products—the FLT and its isolation mounts, the Evo engines large and small, the sporting FXRs—were created or initiated during AMF ownership.

The Sportster, meanwhile, received its own version of the Evolution engine, with alloy top end, as well as a really sharp paint scheme over that classic peanut tank. *Ron Hussey*

Nostalgic? Compare the current Heritage Softail, with its leather-like bags, full fenders, fat front wheel and tire, and even the chromed dome on the front wheel, with the Hydra-Glide of half a century ago.

Soichiro Honda was a visionary, a gearhead, a racer, and a charismatic leader. He had the useful talent of making what he wanted what you wanted. Even so, Honda was careful to credit his full partner, a quiet, self-effacing accountant who knew how to run a business. Honda couldn't have done it without taking care of the business end too.

The gutsy few who hocked their watches and borrowed beyond their limits weren't just men whose names were on the factory or who had spent their working and personal lives involved with motorcycles. The key investors were men who had climbed into the arena wearing AMF uniforms, so to speak, and climbed out in Harley-Davidson jerseys. They were new to motorcycles but they knew finance, production, and marketing, and how to deal with banks and government agencies. However unfashionable it is to say, AMF was the air beneath the eagle's wings.

And it all began in the 1960s.

INDEX

...s by this author that you might enjoy include:

**Illustrated Buyer's Guide:
Harley-Davidson Since 1965**
ISBN: 0-7603-0383-5

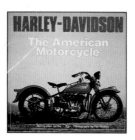

**Harley-Davidson:
The American
Motorcycle**
ISBN: 0-87938-603-7

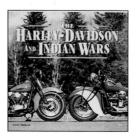

**The Harley-Davidson
and Indian Wars**
ISBN: 0-7603-0208-1

Harley-Davidson
ISBN: 0-7603-0799-7

Other MBI Publishing Company titles of interest:

**101 Harley-Davidson
Performance Projects**
ISBN: 0-7603-03703

**How to Restore Your
Harley-Davidson**
ISBN: 0-87938-934-6

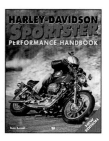

**Harley-Davidson Sportster
Performance Handbook**
ISBN: 0-7603-0307-X

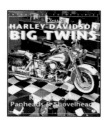

Classic Harley-Davidson Big Twins
ISBN: 0-87938-922-2

Classic Harley-Davidson 1903-1941
ISBN: 0-7603-0557-9

Find us on the internet at www.motorbooks.com   1-800-826-6600